Scale and Distance in Maps

JULIA J. QUINLAN

PowerKiDS press™

New York

Published in 2012 by The Rosen Publishing Group, Inc.
29 East 21st Street, New York, NY 10010

First Edition

Editor: Amelie von Zumbusch
Book Design: Greg Tucker

Photo Credits: Cover, pp. 4, 6, 9, 10, 12, 17, 20–21 © GeoAtlas; p. 5 Jack Hollingsworth/Digital Vision/Thinkstock; pp. 7, 8, 13 (top), 15, 18–19 Shutterstock.com; p. 11 Thierry Dosogne/Getty Images; p. 13 (bottom) Comstock Images/Comstock/Thinkstock; p. 14 © United States National Parks Service; pp. 16, 22 iStockphoto/Thinkstock; p. 19 (main) Maria Teijeiro/Lifesize/Thinkstock.

Library of Congress Cataloging-in-Publication Data

Quinlan, Julia J.
  Scale and distance in maps / by Julia J. Quinlan. — 1st ed.
      p. cm. — (How to use maps)
  Includes index.
  ISBN 978-1-4488-6156-9 (library binding) — ISBN 978-1-4488-6270-2 (pbk.) —
ISBN 978-1-4488-6271-9 (6-pack)
  1. Map reading—Juvenile literature. 2. Map scales—Juvenile literature. I. Title.
  GA151.Q56 2012
  912.01'48—dc23
                                    2011021289

Manufactured in the United States of America

CPSIA Compliance Information: Batch #WW12PK: For Further Information contact Rosen Publishing, New York, New York at 1-800-237-9932

Contents

Understanding Scale and Distance

Maps show towns, countries, or even the whole world on flat pieces of paper. You can tell just by looking at maps that the things on them are shown smaller than they are in real life. After all, a map of the United States that was the same size as the country would be too big

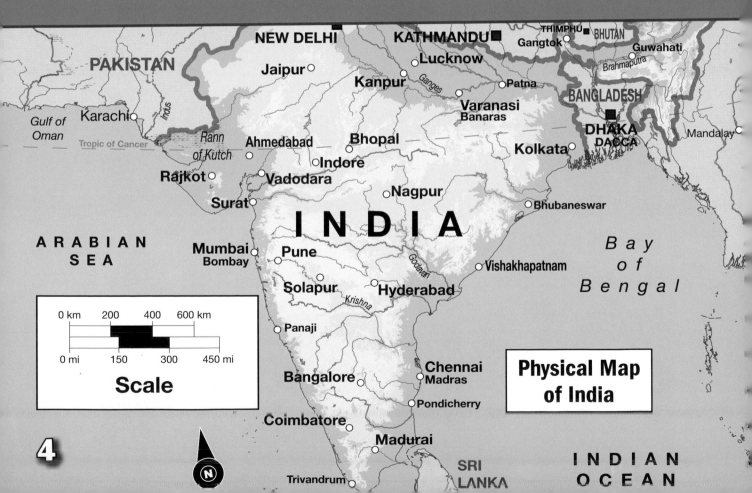

PAKISTAN

NEW DELHI

KATHMANDU

THIMPHU ■ BHUTAN
Gangtok

Guwahati

Jaipur

Lucknow

Brahmaputra

Kanpur

Ganges

Patna

Varanasi
Banaras

BANGLADESH

Gulf of
Oman

Karachi

Indus

Tropic of Cancer

Rann
of Kutch

Ahmedabad

Bhopal

Kolkata

DHAKA
DACCA

Mandalay

Rajkot

Vadodara

Indore

Surat

Nagpur

Bhubaneswar

I N D I A

A R A B I A N
S E A

Mumbai
Bombay

Pune

Godavari

Vishakhapatnam

B a y
o f
B e n g a l

Solapur

Hyderabad

Krishna

Panaji

Scale			
0 km	200	400	600 km
0 mi	150	300	450 mi

Scale

Bangalore

Chennai
Madras

**Physical Map
of India**

Pondicherry

Coimbatore

Madurai

4

N

SRI
LANKA

I N D I A N
O C E A N

Trivandrum

to use. A map's scale tells you how much smaller things are on it than they are in real life.

Maps use different scales depending on how much **information** they show. For example, a map of the whole world uses a different scale from a map of a city.

A map's scale lets you understand how big the distances between things shown on the map really are.

Large Scale and Small Scale

On a map with a small scale, big areas look a lot smaller than they are in real life. A world map is a small-scale map. To fit the whole world on a map, the countries and oceans must be

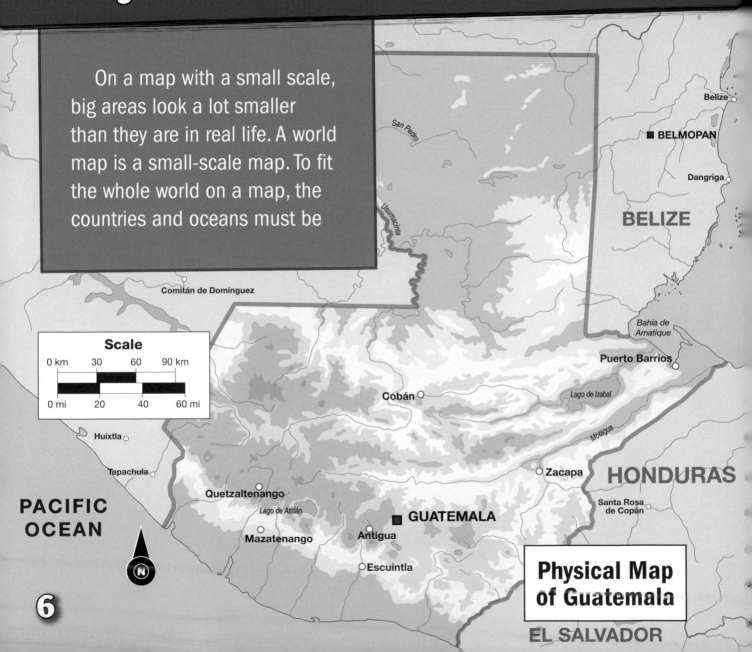

Scale

0 km 30 60 90 km

0 mi 20 40 60 mi

San Pedro

Usumacinta

Comitán de Domínguez

Belize

■ BELMOPAN

Dangriga

BELIZE

Bahía de Amatique

Puerto Barrios

Cobán

Lago de Izabal

Motagua

Huixtla

Tapachula

Zacapa

HONDURAS

Quetzaltenango

Lago de Atitlán

Santa Rosa de Copán

PACIFIC OCEAN

■ **GUATEMALA**

Mazatenango

Antigua

Escuintla

Physical Map of Guatemala

EL SALVADOR

shown much smaller. World maps let you see how big countries and oceans are compared to each other. Towns and small islands are too small to show up on these maps, though.

Large-scale maps are much closer up than small-scale maps. A map of a town is a large-scale map. It shows you a small area but has a lot of **detail**.

The map of Guatemala on page 6 has a fairly small scale. The neighborhood map that the woman is looking at in the picture below has a much larger scale.

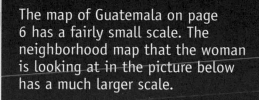

Words, Numbers, and Bars

Maps note their scales in several ways. Many maps use **bar scales**. A bar scale looks like a ruler printed on a map. It is broken up into parts of equal length. The bar scale has numbers along it that show the distances that the equal parts stand for in real life.

Instead of having a bar scale, a map may say 1:250,000. That is a **ratio**. It means

A map's scale helps you understand how far apart things on the map really are. This is useful if you want to get from one place shown on the map to another.

1 inch (2.5 cm) on the map stands for 250,000 inches (635,000 cm) in real life. On some maps, the ratios are written out in words. For example, a map might say "2 inches = 20 miles."

This map uses a bar scale. If it had a ratio, it would read 1:1,000,000. If it used words, it would say "1 cm = 10 km" or "5/8 inch = 10 miles."

TOBAGO

●Scarborough

Physical Map of Trinidad and Tobago

CARIBBEAN SEA

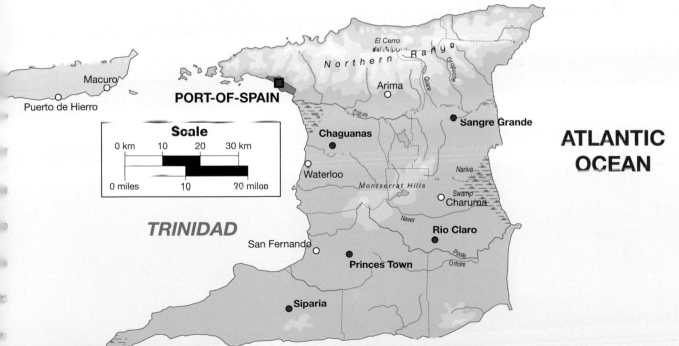

El Cerro

Northern Range

Oropuche

Arima ○

●Sangre Grande

PORT-OF-SPAIN

Macuro ○

Puerto de Hierro ○

Chaguanas ○

ATLANTIC OCEAN

Scale
0 km   10   20   30 km

0 miles   10   20 miles

Waterloo ○

Montserrat Hills

Nariva

Charuma ○

Swamp

Navet

TRINIDAD

San Fernando ○

Rio Claro

Poole

Ortoire

Princes Town

●Siparia

So Many Measurements

Different maps use different units of measurement. You would not measure the inside of a house in miles or kilometers. Houses are not that long! Instead of miles or kilometers, maps of buildings often use feet or meters.

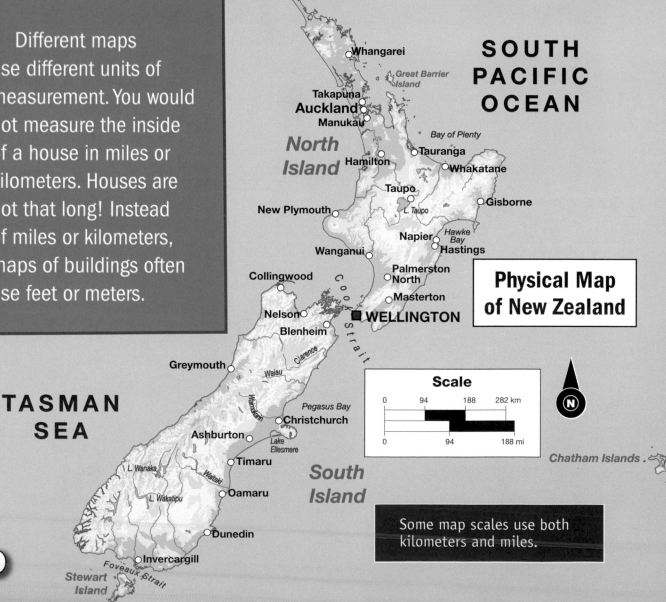

Physical Map of New Zealand

SOUTH PACIFIC OCEAN

Whangarei

Great Barrier Island

Takapuna
Auckland
Manukau

North Island

Bay of Plenty

Hamilton
Tauranga
Whakatane

Taupo
L. Taupo

Gisborne

New Plymouth

Napier
Hawke Bay
Hastings

Wanganui

Palmerston North

Collingwood

Masterton

Nelson
WELLINGTON

Blenheim

Cook Strait

Clarence

Greymouth
Waiau
Waimakariri

Pegasus Bay

TASMAN SEA

Christchurch

Ashburton
Lake Ellesmere

L. Wanaka
Timaru
Waitaki

L. Wakatipu
Oamaru

South Island

Chatham Islands

Dunedin

Invercargill
Foveaux Strait

Stewart Island

Scale

0	94	188	282 km

0	94	188 mi

N

Some map scales use both kilometers and miles.

Distances on maps of countries are measured in miles or kilometers because they are big. Miles are used in the United States. Kilometers are used in countries that use the **metric system**.

Maps of oceans often use **nautical** miles. People who travel by ship often use these maps. When they fly over the ocean, airplane pilots also use maps that measure distance in nautical miles.

This officer is looking at a nautical map. Nautical maps show oceans and other big bodies of water. Their scales often give distances in nautical miles.

Grab Your Ruler

If you want to know how far apart two cities really are, start by measuring the distance between them on the map. A ruler works well for this.

Suppose that two cities on a map measure 5 inches (13 cm) apart. If that map's scale says that 5 inches (13 cm) = 10 miles (16 km), the cities are really 10 miles (16 km) apart.

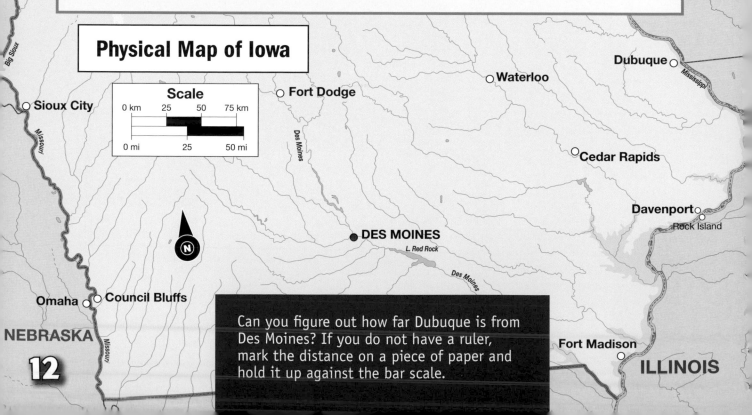

Physical Map of Iowa

Scale

0 km   25   50   75 km

0 mi   25   50 mi

Big Sioux

Sioux City

Missouri

Fort Dodge

Des Moines

Waterloo

Dubuque

Mississippi

Cedar Rapids

Davenport

Rock Island

DES MOINES

L. Red Rock

Des Moines

Omaha

Council Bluffs

NEBRASKA

Missouri

Fort Madison

ILLINOIS

Can you figure out how far Dubuque is from Des Moines? If you do not have a ruler, mark the distance on a piece of paper and hold it up against the bar scale.

If the map says 1:100,000, multiply the distance between the two cities on the map by 100,000. If distance on the map is 5 inches (13 cm), the cities are really 500,000 inches (1,270,000 cm) apart. This **converts** to about 8 miles (13 km).

Left: The direct distance between places is sometimes called the distance as the crow flies. This is because crows can fly in straight lines. They do not have to stick to roads!
Bottom: Rulers are handy for measuring distances on maps.

Unwind Your String

Can you use a string and this map of Catoctin Mountain Park, in Maryland, to figure out how far the hike from the Visitor Center to Blue Ridge Mountain Overlook is?

Rulers are great for measuring straight distances. What if you want to know how long a winding road between two towns is, though? You can use a piece of yarn or string. Lay the yarn along the winding road on the map. Mark off the

Scale

0   0.5   1 Kilometer

0   0.5   1 Mile

CATOCTIN MOUNTAIN PARK
(National Park Service)

Sawmill

Owens Creek
Browns Farm Trail

Poplar Grove

Chestnut
Spicebush Nature Trail

Blue Ridge Summit Overlook
1520ft
463m

1880ft
573m

Foxville

Round Meadow

Greentop

Park Central Road

Charcoal Trail

Thurmont Vista
1499ft
457m

Hog Rock Nature Trail

Hog Rock
1610ft
491m

Misty Mount Cabins
(reservations needed)

Manahan Road

Catoctin Trail

Big Hunting Creek

77

Accessibility parking only

Blue Blazes Whiskey Still

Falls Nature Trail

Visitor Center
920ft/280m

Wolf Rock
1401ft
427m

Cunningham Falls

William Houck Area

Snack bar
Boat rental

Hunting Creek Lake

Dam

Store

Boat launch
Fishing pier

Chimney Rock
1419ft
432m

Catoctin Mountain Park Headquarters
840ft
256m

Frank Bentz Memorial Lake

Campground registration
Dump station

Bear Branch

Foxville Road

Sabillasville Road

Western Maryland Railroad

550

77

15

two towns on it. Then straighten the yarn out. If the map has a bar scale, lay the string on top of it to see how long the road is.

If the map has a ratio in words or numbers, measure the string with a ruler. Then use math to figure out what the distance is in real life.

Roads take winding paths for many reasons. For example, some roads curve to make their way around a mountain. Roads wind to make their way up mountains, too.

Grids

Some maps have **grids**. Grids are made up of evenly spaced lines running **horizontally** and **vertically**. A grid's lines make a series of boxes. Every box on a map grid is the same size. If you know how long each square of the grid is, you can use the grid to **estimate**, or guess, distance. This comes in handy if you do not have anything with which to measure the distance.

Grid boxes are often labeled with numbers or letters. This makes it easy to describe where things are on a map with a grid. Just tell someone which square to look in!

Grids are useful for drawing maps, too. Scientists make rope grids when they find fossils, such as these bones. They use the grids to draw maps that show how the fossils were arranged.

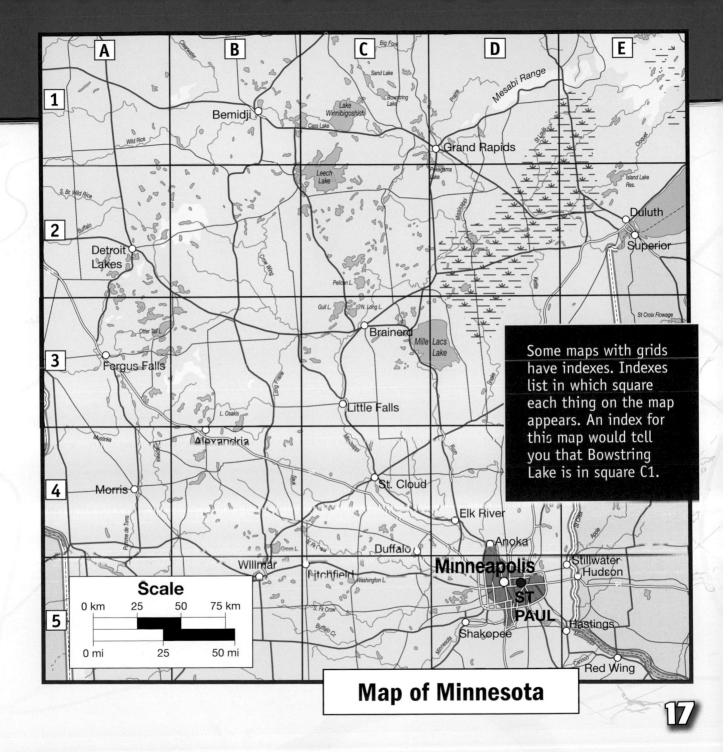

Some maps with grids have indexes. Indexes list in which square each thing on the map appears. An index for this map would tell you that Bowstring Lake is in square C1.

Scale

0 km 25 50 75 km

0 mi 25 50 mi

Map of Minnesota

Let's Plan a Trip!

If you know how fast you hike, you can use a map to figure out how long a hike will take, too.

Maps help you find the best way to get to a place. They can also help you figure out how long it will take to get there.

Want to know how long it would take to drive from one city to another? Look at a map and measure how far apart the two cities are. You also need to know how fast the car would be traveling. If the cities are 120 miles (193 km) apart and the car is going 60 miles per hour (97 km/h), the trip will take 2 hours. This is because 120 divided by 60 is 2.

It is a good idea to use a map to work out how long your trip will take before you leave. If you do not, you could be late!

How Big Is It Really?

It is hard for world maps to show the world as it really is. Earth is round not flat. When it is flattened to show it on a map, it can become **distorted**. Sometimes countries will not be the right shape or size when compared to others.

One type of world map, called the Mercator map, makes Africa and Greenland look the same size. In real life, Africa is 14 times larger than Greenland. The Peters map and other equal-area maps show the true areas of places. However, the shapes of things are a little distorted on these maps.

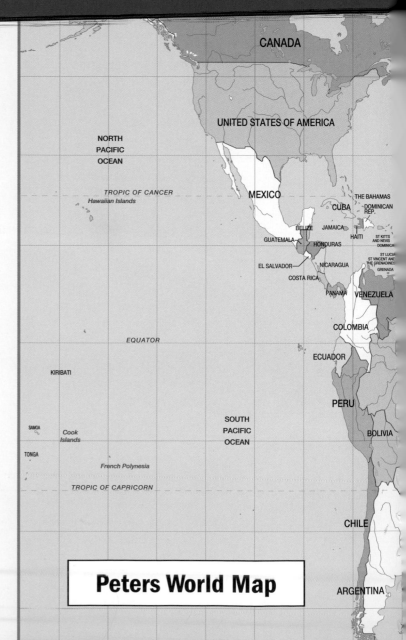

Peters World Map

RUSSIAN FEDERATION

KAZAKHSTAN

MONGOLIA

NORTH
KOREA

NORTH
PACIFIC
OCEAN

UNITED
KINGDOM
SWEDEN
ESTONIA
DENMARK
LATVIA
LITHUANIA
IRELAND
NETHERLANDS
BELGIUM
POLAND
BELARUS
LUXEMBOURG
UKRAINE
SWITZERLAND
FRANCE
ITALY
ROMANIA
MOLDOVA
ANDORRA
VATICAN CITY
BULGARIA
GEORGIA
UZBEKISTAN
KYRGYZSTAN
SPAIN
MACEDONIA
ARMENIA
AZERB.
TAJIKISTAN
ALBANIA
CYPRUS
TURKMENISTAN
PORTUGAL
GREECE
TURKEY
SYRIA
AFGHANISTAN
CHINA
MALTA
LEBANON
WEST BANK
IRAQ
IRAN
KASHMIR
JAPAN
SOUTH
KOREA
TAIWAN

NORTH
ATLANTIC
OCEAN

TROPIC OF CANCER

TUNISIA

MOROCCO

ALGERIA

LIBYA

EGYPT

ISRAEL
JORDAN
KUWAIT
BAHRAIN
QATAR
U.A.E.

SAUDI
ARABIA

OMAN

PAKISTAN

NEPAL
BHUTAN
BANGLADESH

INDIA

MYANMAR
(BURMA)
LAOS

THAILAND

VIETNAM

CAMBODIA

TROPIC OF CANCER

WESTERN
SAHARA

MAURITANIA

MALI

NIGER

CHAD

SUDAN

ERITREA

DJIBOUTI

YEMEN

MARSHALL
ISLANDS

ANTIGUA AND BARBUDA

CAPE VERDE

SENEGAL

GAMBIA

GUINEA-BISSAU
GUINEA

BURKINA
FASO
NIGERIA

BENIN

SIERRA LEONE

CÔTE
D'IVOIRE
GHANA
TOGO

CENTRAL
AFRICAN
REPUBLIC

SOUTH
SUDAN

ETHIOPIA

SOMALIA

PHILIPPINES

FEDERATED STATES
OF MICRONESIA

BARBADOS

TRINIDAD AND TOBAGO

GUYANA

SURINAME

FRENCH
GUIANA

LIBERIA

CAMEROON

SRI LANKA

MALDIVES

PALAU

BRUNEI
MALAYSIA

EQUATOR

EQUAT. GUINEA

SÃO TOMÉ
AND PRÍNCIPE
GABON

CONGO

RWANDA

UGANDA

KENYA

BURUNDI

EQUATOR

INDONESIA

PAPUA
NEW GUINEA

NAURU

BRAZIL

DEM. REP.
OF THE CONGO

TANZANIA

SEYCHELLES

INDIAN
OCEAN

EAST TIMOR

SOLOMON
ISLANDS

SOUTH
ATLANTIC
OCEAN

ANGOLA

ZAMBIA

MALAWI

COMOROS

MAURITIUS

VANUATU

PARAGUAY

TROPIC OF CAPRICORN

NAMIBIA

BOTSWANA

ZIMBABWE

MOZAMBIQUE

MADAGASCAR

TROPIC OF CAPRICORN

AUSTRALIA

SWAZILAND

URUGUAY

LESOTHO

SOUTH AFRICA

Scale at the Equator

| 0 km | 1000 | 2000 | 3000 km |

| 0 mi | 1000 | 2000 mi |

SOUTHERN OCEAN

NEW ZEALAND

21

Big World and Small Map

If you compare maps, check to see if they use the same scale. This is important even when you are looking at a world **atlas**. This is a book that has maps of every country in the world. A map of a small country, such as Belize, would likely be at a different scale from a map of the United States.

From kilometers to ratios, there are many things to know about scale and distance in maps. Knowing about scale and distance makes maps easier to understand.

If you are using a map, make sure to check its scale. Otherwise, you will not know if something on the map is 1 mile (2 km) away or 10 miles (16 km) away!

Glossary

atlas (AT-lus) A book of maps.

bar scales (BAHR SKAYLZ) Tools that are drawn on maps to show what distances on the maps are in real life.

converts (kun-VERTS) Changes something into a different form.

detail (dih-TAYL) Having lots of small parts.

distorted (dih-STAWRT-ed) Having a shape or size that is twisted or changed from its original shape or size.

estimate (ES-teh-mayt) To make a guess based on knowledge or facts.

grids (GRIDZ) Patterns of evenly spaced lines running up and down and across.

horizontally (hor-ih-ZON-til-ee) Going from side to side.

information (in-fer-MAY-shun) Knowledge or facts.

metric system (MEH-trik SIS-tem) A method of measurement based on counting tens.

nautical (NAW-tih-kul) Having to do with ships or sailors.

ratio (RAY-shoh) The way a size difference between two or more objects is shown.

vertically (VER-tih-kul-ee) Going up and down.

Index

Web Sites

Due to the changing nature of Internet links, PowerKids Press has developed an online list of Web sites related to the subject of this book. This site is updated regularly. Please use this link to access the list:

www.powerkidslinks.com/maps/scale/